The Angel of Duluth

The Angel of Duluth

Madelon Sprengnether

The Marie Alexander Poetry Series, Volume 9
Series Editor: Robert Alexander

WHITE PINE PRESS / BUFFALO, NEW YORK

WHITE PINE PRESS
P.O. Box 236
Buffalo, New York 14201

Acknowledgments:
"Apology" appeared in *Caprice*. "La Belle et la Bête (after Jean Cocteau)," "La
Belle et la Bête, Take 2," "La Belle et la Bête, Outtake 1" and "La Belle et la Bête,
Outtake 2" appeared in *Southern Lights:* PEN South Anthology, vol. 2, 1998.
"The Franklin Avenue Bridge" and "Mars and Venus (after Botticelli)" appeared
in *The Talking of Hands: A Thirtieth Anniversary Celebration,* eds. Robert Alexander,
Mark Vinz and C.W. Truesdale (New Rivers Press, 1998).

The following poems were published in chapbook form, under the title *La Belle
et La Bête* (Sarasota Poetry Theater Press, 1999): "La Belle et la Bête (after Jean
Cocteau)," "La Belle et la Bête, Take 2," "La Belle et la Bête, Take 3," "La Belle
et la Bête, Take 4," "La Belle et la Bête, Take 5," "La Belle et la Bête, Outtake 1,"
"La Belle et la Bête, Outtake 2," "La Belle et la Bête, Outtake 3," "Lake," "Lake
2," "Lake 3," "Lake 4," "Lake 5," "Lake 6," "Lake 7," "Lake 8," "The Subject
of Angels," "The Franklin Avenue Bridge," "Notre Dame de Bonsecours," "The
Angel of Duluth," "The Angel of Duluth 2," "The Angel of Duluth 3," "The
Angel of Duluth 4," "Annunciation."

Publication of this book was made possible by support from Robert
Alexander and with public funds from the New York State
Council on the Arts, a State Agency.

First Edition.

10-digit ISBN: 1-893996-48-4
13-digit ISBN: 978-1-83996-48-9

Printed and bound in the United States of America.

Library of Congress Control Number: 2005934743

For Ilse

Contents

Anniversary

Lake

La Belle et la Bête

Lot's Wife

The Angel of Duluth

The Angel of Duluth

Anniversary

Anniversary

I

It was muggy and hot, one of those days when the air feels as close as your own breath. The garden we had prepared was green with the beginnings of things that would grow wild over the summer. No iris, peonies, or tiger lilies yet, the raspberry canes barely covering their thorns. We were so new we might have been naked, standing in front of our friends, our hands moist with love and full of promises. "Oh you, you are like the hart in the forest, your thighs fragrant with cedar, your hair like hyacinths." "And you, you are like a waterfall that spills from the mountains, your breasts pools of quiet, your navel a honeycomb," we said, the words tumbling from our mouths.

2

I lied a little. There are things I don't want to tell you. How lonely I am today and sick at heart. How the rain falls steadily and cold on a garden grown greener, more lush and even less tame. I haven't done much, I confess, to contain it. The grapevine, as usual, threatens everything in its path, while the raspberry canes, aggressive and abundant, are clearly out of control. I'm afraid the wildflowers have taken over, being after all the most hardy and tolerant of shade and neglect. This year the violets and lilies of the valley are rampant, while the phlox are about to emit their shocking pink perfume. Oh, my dear, had you been here this spring, you would have seen how the bleeding hearts are thriving.

Anger

How quickly it leaps out, like snakes or frogs, from our mouths. A swarm of warty creatures that slither and bite. "So do you plan to have another affair?" you challenge me on the street. "No," I shout back, grabbing you by the shoulders to make my point. "Get this through your thick skull," I add, jabbing my fingers at your temples, then stepping back, suddenly abashed. We stand there on the sidewalk, a late middle-aged couple, too stymied to care what kind of spectacle we make. "If you don't love me," I say, choking back tears and snot, "I want you to divorce me." "I don't want to hurt you," you say wearily, as you turn and walk away.

Apology

I kept getting lost near Harvard Square, going off on a tangent,
which wasn't at all, at all what I meant. And then retracing my
steps—in the rain that wouldn't let up and soaked through my
sandals—stopping to consult a map and trying a new tack.
Eventually, I found you, or your office at least, unlocked but
empty. What could I make of such temporary quarters? Of the
stack of unopened mail on your desk—with the exception of one
fat envelope from a dating service, ripped impatiently across the
top? You want to go home, you said, to California, to your
friends, your therapist, before you can decide what is best. It's not
that I don't love you," you offered, with a hard look.

Rain

Everywhere it rains. In California, the most miserable winter you can remember, even worse than the one when the delta seeped and mushed and everything vertical slid downhill, hanging precariously over the ocean. All things porous leaked, the upstairs balcony, the dining room ceiling, especially the ancient garage roof. A long, slow hemorrhage that felt to you like your own body slit open and badly stapled together. Even the hole in your mouth, where that cracked tooth was extracted, weeped and oozed. No wonder then that you cried, slumping over the driving wheel of your car, as if the water flowing from your own openings spewed from the same inexhaustible source.

Reunion

It was old times, smiling and remembering and touching hands in the Italian restaurant, warm air blowing in from the street. You met me at the airport, helped me with my bags, guided me, through market streets strewn with cabbage leaves, carrot tops, and onions, to this place. Thinner after months of separation, we both looked younger. We might have passed for tourists, honeymooners, or even first-time lovers. I read the difference in your eyes, the pupils black as bullet holes. Over dinner, as we talked, they kept growing wider, like a source of gravity that pulls matter to its core. Sucking everything—even light—into its vanishing well.

Hope

How do you calibrate hope? In a relaxation around the eyes, a vibration in the voice, a hand that hovers lightly under my fingertips? That last evening, over dinner, you were in a mood for joking. No doubt a good sign. But I've lost all confidence in my powers of translation. You are like the French I once knew but haven't spoken in years, full of tricky vowels and false cognates. How miraculous then that we slipped, for one iridescent moment, back into each other's idiom, conjuring love like a children's game.

Letter to my Nearly Ex-husband

Are you in Perugia or Venice? And is it humid and overcast? As it was on our honeymoon in Rome, Assisi, Florence? I can't help thinking of you, of our heated love and frantic innocence. Here it's oppressive, the sky dark as lead. Random streaks of lightning and fatal accidents on the freeway, but no relief from the weight of August, with its shrill cicadas, its atmosphere of moist threat. Do you call to me—as I to you—in the middle of the night, struggling through nightmares in which I sweat and sweat? Why aren't you here with me, trembling through the violence of a tornado alert? Why aren't you with me now as this relentless storm drives its stakes over and over into the ground?

I'm Leaving You

I'm leaving you now. I can feel it. How silence muffles and diminishes—like a train sounding a mournful warning in the small hours before dawn. Or like those tiny figures in the upper reaches of Renaissance paintings. How did you let me travel so far without you? Why did you turn your back at that last fork, not even looking at me—so intent on reaching the next stage of ascent? How could I have known, the day we tried to scramble up a stretch of scree in Yosemite, that we would never arrive at the summit? That, on descending in a sudden, cold, driving rain, we would each harbor another wish, another secret map in our hearts?

You Surprise Yourself

In your fifties, you seem too old for this. For this heaving, buck-
ling, ugly eruption in your life. It's crude and, quite frankly,
embarrassing. You feel, in the nakedness of your loss, like Hamlet's
mother, caught in some randy act—lifting your legs, your red-
dened crotch with its thinning hairs, for the whole world to snig-
ger at. Yet, in the full, grunting, expression of your grief, you no
longer care how you look. Instead, everything you have ever want-
ed to hide comes pouring out—like some ancient burst water
main—full of floating particles and rust.

The Change

They say this change is like a death. Something that focuses your awareness of what you have lost. Your youth, for instance, with its simple and hopeful uncertainties. The choices you might have made, but didn't—lives you might have lived, but couldn't. Something shrivels now, they say, something dessicates. Mummy-like, you begin to contract. People will see this—in the bleached and paperish quality of your skin, your hair. You are like something preserved, at best, in a dry climate, which will turn to ash if exposed to light and air. Why, then, this sudden sense of flowing? Why this passion for water in all forms of movement? For still calm—and churning release.

Lake

Lake

I

How do I love you? Let me count the ways. Bird migration in
spring. Suddenly—blue heron, coot, Canada goose, merganser.
They flutter the water, then dip out of sight in its chill smooth-
ness. So sleek that it reflects light like old silver. Near the shore I
can see large, rounded stones, gleaming a midnight blue, dull sage
or ochre. I wake at night to this shadowy paleness, like a thin
plate brimming with soup. Who holds you, I wonder, in the
scoop of one hand? You are my solace and my terror. You are the
dark question mark that surges briefly into the air, falling into
the deep.

2

In the winter, it was fixed, immobile. A single mass that revealed its force by pushing up, inches thick, at the shore. It was strong enough to crack wood, uprooting steps and docks, leaving them beached and helpless. And yet the palest of light played over its surface, as if to say that such brute pressure could also be delicate. Rich with pinks and every shade of peach and lavender, this heaving mass of white that could burn your naked flesh called to something more obscure. Wetter. Deeper. Sunken into slow-moving torpor. You knew it was there. Waiting.

3

Light, liquidity, and movement set me adrift. No matter the season or time of day, once my eyes stray toward water, I begin to feel sleepy and unintelligent. My mind searching only for images. What can this simple, rocking motion be like? As each cross-hatched ripple hastens toward the shore, I think of the hand-stitching on a quilt, the work of patient fingers that see only the path before them. A series of tiny, surfacing and diving movements—like fish that break the water's milky skin. Rising and falling, a pulse that never misses a syncopated beat. Occult but alive. Something that loves me.

4

It's a long muscle, isn't it? This bright, silvery form that leaps into the air, shaking itself briefly, then slapping back into the water. Why such sudden activity, so late in the day? Some only nudging the surface of the water, some more ambitious. Launching themselves at an oblique angle, as if to taste this odd, even heady, environment more fully. The most dazzling take the risk of annihilation, like acrobats on a high wire, knowing their next move may precipitate a fall like no other. A surge that shivers along the whole length of shining skin. Random. Wilding.

5

This summer I swam in it. Slowly lowering my body to the horizontal, then wetting my hair, moving my limbs, and immersing all my frontal openings. Warm and silky, it whispered to me of yellow/brown/greenish life in places I couldn't see, much less imagine. I mistrusted this—as anyone should. Who knows what cool depths lay below, what sly eddies or currents might ensnare me? Yet the sky shone blue as a baby's eye, and as I rocked in its reflection I dreamed of my life as some mild, slippery thing that could dive or rise—like the shapes fleeing past me, grazing me here and there. Like a lover's touch.

6

I walk alone, this time, in another season. I can tell by the colors. Not gray and green as in the spring, overcast and rainy—nor brazen and effulgently blue, as in the summer with its flashes of white-hot brilliance. Cerulean rather and copper-gold—as in oak leaves littering the ground, the sky as smooth and calm as the lake. Which hardly ripples—yet oscillates, so you know there's something alive and moving just below the surface. The geese cry early now, as they stretch their wings for the long flight away from here. And the smells along the path of decay—like small, yellow-red crabapples blending sweetishly into the earth.

7

No ducks or geese today in the soft ice pools remaining. Even last week a few from under the bridge fluttered a brief protest, then picked their way across the packed surface to glide into the water's lucid chill. They are gone, like my front porch geraniums shriveled after a hard frost. Now only stiff, spiky wheat, the color of rust and blood. Like the cattails and marsh grasses, hissing their dark secrets. Trees hunch together along the horizon, blue-black and suspicious. While overhead, sharp-billed crows utter harsh-throated, bronchial cries.

8

It's the pearly delicacy of winter that moves me. The late after-
noon sky the sheerest pink, like gauze from a little girl's tutu.
Shading toward lavender at the tree line and banked like smoke.
It's borderline now, some days freezing, some days melting, the
ice advancing and receding from the shore. Water flows, swift and
narrow under the bridge, black with amber glints between the
rustling grasses, the bleached and crusting snow. Winter has no
discretion, a body without embarrassment or shame. As if to say,
in this light, even a bruise or blood-mark is beautiful.

9

The light before dawn is boring. The sky like dirty dishwater, the snow a flat, sheet-like expanse. No discernible difference between the land and the lake. Even the tree-line a gunmetal streak. Listless light. A profile of mourning. But then slowly in the east, a luminosity that shifts the sky into hues of mauve, lavender, silver. The snow too begins to flush and glow, rising in rose-gold dunes with purplish hollows. This is what it means to be patient.

10

Winter, I have always said, is not my season. My fingers dry and electric, my fingertips papery and white, my words congealing into cartoon clouds even as I speak. But this morning, a suffusion of peach from somewhere east of here. Then a brighter, hotter orange, a liquidity that melts the air, causing even the hard carapace of ice to vibrate, to undulate. A fire lit somewhere under the earth. The sun a clot of gold spit from its seething heart.

II

Snow-waves across the lake, the light a lemon-peach with blue shadows running leeward. So often now this landscape reminds me of the desert—the exposed sky, the fine dry air, the silence. A seduction so pure that it could lure you into a final, wintry embrace. It would bite first, so that your skin ached and throbbed. Then you would forget to feel with your extremities. You would become a clear, stinging consciousness, filled with this dazzle of color, from pale persimmon through the sun's hot palette. You would fall in love with the burning snow. You could relinquish the small glitter of yourself.

12

Beginnings and endings are most dramatic—the lake splintery white, overlaid with a sharp coppery color and slanting shadows. Still the ground seems kinder than the sky, so bright it pains your eyes—an acid blue edged with gold. It's early January, the unfiltered light as immediate as a bare electric bulb. Today, it's at least 20 below. Days like these are what you have feared. Like a mirror or magnifying glass, they intensify and expose. They hold you mesmerized, like the shards of ice you find on the path, darting their fierce, tiny rainbows. These days flash before your eyes like a switchblade knife, unflinching and true.

La Belle et la Bête

La Belle et la Bête (after Jean Cocteau)

I

There were too many symbols from the start. This I should have
seen, driving up in the dark, with all those lights pointing like
arrows to your house. Once inside, I couldn't help marveling how
everything was laid out—food and clothing—exactly suited to
my purpose. Even the mirror you offered smoked and cleared,
deepening into my past. But what you really wanted was to watch,
tracking my every move, like some hidden camera, some retail-
store video device. There was a crime at issue, some bloody viola-
tion, some pain of death. Every night you would stand at my
bedroom door, pleading and anguished. "I'm not an animal," you
would say, "don't look at me like that."

2

When does the castle grow ugly? When the price of a single rose is tallied, or later? Which is worse: that a growing thing may be owned, that a life may be exacted? Or that a young girl's longing for a father should thwart her marriage prospects? Each is drawn to the other, like iron filings to a magnet. He is full of slavering hunger, his need so raw he doesn't even use his hands to feed. She flinches, claws at her skirt, oh so delicately appalled. Some days, she feels the weight of his gaze like a chain of pearls suspended from her neck. Yet she did this of her own volition. In the cloudless pool of her mind, she cannot form the idea of escape.

3

I can't get it out of my mind, how naked you were, both hairy
and shorn, as if itching to be free of your very skin. Angry red
blotches would appear on your back and chest, which you
scratched at, as if to shed such a useless casing. You were like
something in metamorphosis, writhing in confinement. I did not
want to witness this. Nothing in my life had prepared me for
such a lack—of simple modesty or adornment. Later, I would
stand at the mirror, smoothing my hands over breasts and hips,
pleased by the clear contours of my reflection. Feeling along my
shivering flesh for the slightest tremors of agitation.

4

She believes they are different species. Though sprung from the same salt matrix, their genes must long ago have diverged, so that no one would now dream of linking their fates. Why then does she feel no fear in his presence; how to comprehend her own boldness? She longs only for what came before; once released, why honor a bargain with the devil? Time was, her compassion would rise at the simple spectacle of his suffering—as easy as caring for a sick pet. Now she knows better. What pulls her back has nothing to do with innocence or experience. It is the violence of his extremity she relishes.

5

She is used to obeying—not speaking in her own voice. To arrive
at this place, I have had to subordinate myself. She has accepted
so much. None of it what I wanted. Now that she is mute, I can
hear/see everything. How her father is dying, how the beast will
die also. How I want to save\love them both. How she will
always be torn between this one and that. To love each in turn
might offer some solace, but this requires more than she has
strength for. If there is anything like salvation I think it must feel
like sadness—so protracted, so real, so deep that no one can live
to the end of it. Least of all her; least of all me.

6

I want an end to this story. One that will satisfy him, will satisfy me. But these are romances—where the two of them rise through spun-sugar clouds in some candied dream of sexual ecstasy. What we know of each other is more crude, somber and urgent. I want to say something like this. That, yes, I loved you—even when I appeared to be cool or impassive. It was your hurt that moved me. What I loved most was your *laideur*, the very parts of yourself that you hated, the parts you were sure that no one could cherish. It's how we are alike.

La Belle et la Bête, Outtakes

I

Things I never told you. How sitting on your lap, with your cock pushed hard up inside me, I would lose all sense of decorum. It wasn't a question of how I was raised, but how I felt reduced to this one overwhelming sensation. This is not love, I thought, it is something more primitive. How I understood your body's secrets and vulnerabilities. I had only to open my mouth for you to open yours, your tongue lithe and available. This is what bound me to you—the sign of your helplessness. And then the ultimate pleasure, the knowledge that I could move you to that place where you had no will. No choice but to give.

2

You begged me to hurt you. And you meant it—physically.
"This pain," you said, "is so exquisite." I was ashamed, not want-
ing to admit how easy it was to harm—to twist your nipples, to
rake my nails along your skin, gouging them into your back, your
buttocks. How I could not speak my own desire, it was so enor-
mous, like the bulk of your mass pressing me against the smooth,
flat-sheeted bed. I liked it best when you forced yourself so rap-
idly inside me that my breath came in bursts, my body making
sharp cries. Learning this was the hardest thing. How strange I
was to myself. Like you, I was capable of anything.

3

I want to say something true. But I splinter like ice when I begin
to form the simplest of thoughts. Such as: I loved you/it was all
my fault/something prevented me from giving what you asked.
Let me try again. It wasn't that I didn't love you, it was something
more acute. Like the hope\hopelessness of childhood. But I'm
boring you—you're wondering why I can't get to the point. My
dear, it wasn't about what you did or didn't do; it was about my
own limit. The snarl of wish and desire you aroused in me.
Straddling you until you were lathered and spent/or crouching
and quivering like a bitch in heat.

Lot's Wife

Rebecca (after Alfred Hitchcock)

I

What he loved in her was her not knowing. It was some image of himself he could barely recall—all shyness, soft withdrawal and reticence. Surely, as a child, he must have experienced this. She could release him of all culpability—through her sheer transparence. More than her pliant and simply cleaving flesh, what he desired was the wholeness of her thought. Which he pictured as freshly laundered bed sheets, snapping in the wind on a brisk day in March. She was as free as she was supple, as easily excited as quiescent. How he longed to pour himself, like a filmed and stagnant pool, into her clear chalice.

2

She knows what he wanted, what he has done. She can forgive him this, or anything. She wants him for her own and will sacrifice what she must to have him—even her girlish memory. Such love, she believes, has nothing to do with domesticity or any of the household virtues, like compassion. It is visceral, opening her bowels or cramping her stomach like a fist. She feels him move in her like history. She would lie with him anywhere—even in the cold, coastal waters of his thought. If only he would permit her this luxury.

Lot's Wife (for Mona Van Duyn)

You saw it so clearly, that terrible moral of punishment and shame. How the men, nervous and obsessed, worry over judgment, when the gist of the story lies elsewhere—the legacy of a woman with no name. Who should care which organ goes into which orifice, the sum of humiliation or sorrow, who did what to whom? The angels, those honored guests, would sacrifice anyone to save themselves. A crime worse than you would have believed. This is what caused you to mourn, relinquishing your own hopes and wishes. Someone, you felt, should pay respect to the flawed, perishable, human past.

Mars and Venus (after Botticelli)

Does anyone wonder what they've been up to? He reclining, as relaxed as a baby and as carelessly naked, except for the cloth slung low on the groin—the right hand slack and open in the place of his sex. One knee raised, exposing a long white inner thigh, the throat equally girlish and abandoned. No need for helmet or lance—toys now for baby fauns' play. She is at ease also. But half upright, calmly awake, and fully clothed. Her breasts accentuated by a braid-like band that defines sleeves and neckline, her hair both loose and plaited. His lips are parted; hers are closed. He is lost in sleep; she gazes toward something off-frame, pondering the inexplicable, next thing.

Ghosts

When the winds came up and the sirens blared, causing me to rouse you from your naked sleep, and we huddled together under an afghan in the blue glare of the TV, trying to figure the odds on a tornado, hearing the storm roar over us with gale force, while upstairs shades began flapping and a door slammed shut, I said "Don't worry, it's just the ghost." Joking. Later, when you called from another coast telling me that you want to see me, but somewhere "neutral," where there are no restless spirits, I said "I'm sorry, but where I go they go—like Ruth and Naomi." When someone departs it's all right to be haunted. How else would you know you were missed?

The Pillow Book (after Peter Greenaway)

In mid-June, death exhales a steamy, rotten breath. Just today there was another body found in the river. A young man, thirty-ish, with curly brown hair (already thinning and receding), wearing blue-jean shorts and a tee shirt with a Hawaiian greeting. He hadn't been in the water long, bumping gently against the Mississippi shore. At this time of year, everything swells and exudes quickly, blurring the most identifiable parts. Can such a lumpish thing be turned to art? The skin skimmed and bleached into a fine, paperish texture. Good for some kind of message. Not readable but tactile. To wrap ourselves in as loss dissolves our bones. Something to make us believe in our names.

Necrophilia

In this movie a woman is in love with the body of death. She wants to smell, touch, taste it. She wants to puncture it, caressing the internal organs, watching the exchange of chemicals with blood. If she sings, dances, has sex with it, she will feel its whole history of hurt or joy. For such a thrill, she is willing to do anything. But this is fiction. Tonight, in Sally's kitchen, I hear a woman describe how she entered her mother's bedroom moments after her death. How the air in there was like mica, thin and flashing. Yet how warm and supple her mother's flesh. How she washed her, changed her nightgown, combed her hair. How she inhaled then, deeply and slowly. Taking into her lungs all the cutting edges of her life.

At Night

All kinds of disturbance. Clatter in my bedroom, like clothes
hangers falling. Then pressure on my body, both heavy and
light—like smoke from a fire made with damp twigs. Next,
someone I don't recognize, pushing into me from behind. Then
my ex-husband, loving me the way he never did. Once it was a
girl who wanted to lie beside me. They crowd in when I'm out
cold, defenseless. I heard a story once about a ghost who came to
appraise every guest who stayed in the house. But I have too
many. Even my telephone—emitting little yips—is far too
excitable. What will it cost me to make you go? Wilder nights?
More uproar?

Equinox

This night is full of contradictions—soft snow, blowing hard.
Full blizzard weather at the year's slip cog from winter to spring.
Higher and higher it piles, like layer upon layer of white icing.
Or a froth of spun sugar that melts at the touch of your tongue.
Today, after dreaming the possibility of lilacs blossoming in my
bare yard, I broke down and cried. In a pure white-out, I forgot
everything. How, like a tight bulb, I had carried myself through
the long winter. How even in this smooth landscape of grief
there lies hidden a trick bird or rabbit, waiting for a child's dis-
cerning eye. How the earth, just now, makes a hairspring turn
toward the sun.

The Angel of Duluth

Notre Dame de Bonsecours

We saw you from a distance, on a rain-slashed autumn morning in Montreal. Looking for the old town, aiming for your somber beacon. A lead-gray figure leaning over the water, a wire-like contraption fixed over your head, dotted with stars. Off the cobblestone street, we push through double wooden doors. Inside, a little world, with more statues in niches, paintings, candles, hanging lamps in the shape of sailing ships. All bathed in a delicate blue light from the dome behind the altar, a luminous aqua shell, with more points of silver for stars. What is *bonsecours* but good help when we need it? At any time of day or night, in all kinds of weather. Like a pair of raw-boned hands held open to the river. To the sleepless, tantrum-driven sea.

On the Subject of Angels

Today is the feast of guardian angels, says the gentle, diffident priest. Do we want to talk about this? Angels make me think of falling—as in Milton's *Paradise Lost.* A dark radiance, like sulphur from a burning match. Like the earth's core? I once bought an orange sapphire—for the strangeness of its color. It was February, when the snow was packed and sooty underfoot. The world looked too much like ash. I wanted a little fire to wear on my hand to remind me of the myriad possibilities of heat. If I have an angel, she must be like Emily Dickinson—solitary, uncompromising, but neither cool nor remote. No silvery, watery reflection, white on white on white. My angel her own Vesuvius. Raging light.

The Angel of Duluth

I

I couldn't resist her, she was so light. So simple even—a blue bunting gown, small cone-shaped bowl held just below her breast, and pointy, fan-like wings. She might even be a boy or lovely man, with her long yellow hair and reddish lips. I could have had my pick of madonnas, gilded with hope or sorrow. This angel was different, bearing her carefully clasped gift. When she fell and broke clean through I learned her secret. She was all airy inside, full of holes, like something eaten by tree-boring insects. She harbored her emptiness like a honeycomb—full of desire and portent.

2

She wasn't sure what she beheld, why she was sad, or what she was hugging in her basket. Her eyes cast inward, contemplative. She neither flew nor stood, but seemed to hover, suspended. Was she trying to ascend? I don't think so. She seemed earthbound— like the yellow moon, held in orbit by invisible bands. If she could speak, she might say she was not the rising kind. As if to say, I won't leave you—and return—and leave you again, like him, always promising, then vanishing. Her greatest wish was more warm-blooded, human. She wanted to be remembered. Having no tongue, she knew she could neither come nor go in flames.

3

Have you noticed her expression? Her eyes off-kilter, large and mascaraed, one higher than the other. Her mouth a rosebud, sweetly pursed, her hands rough in comparison—like a bas-relief on the vessel she carries, a golden triangle, slightly raised above her abdomen. When she cracked, revealing her ingrained faults, I was inconsolable. "If you can heal her," I said, "I will love you forever." Like some goosey girl in a story by Grimm. By the work of your hands I believed I would know you. Paying no heed to the weather in your eyes—to the prickling of my flesh, the chill wind rising.

4

To all appearances, she is intact. The wood filler, the uneven paint a perfect, blue-black match. How can I not see this as one of love's labors? How I asked you to do this, how you relished this task, performing it beyond my wildest wishes. Now no one can see how she was hurt, her hairline fractures invisible to all but an X-ray eye. Like Henry James' fabled bowl—surely a parable of sorts. Yet I can still feel the ache in my shoulder socket, where I once slammed my arm into the pavement. As I can discern the thin, dark line that shows where this angel fell—spilling all her golden contents.

Annunciation

When you are plain and empty, like a bare room with a dirt floor. When you are naked, even a little raw, your skin goose-pimpled from the cold. When you have no thought of exaltation, nothing but the bony scaffolding of your own body, the flimsy dressing of your skin. When your eyes are lowered, not from humility but from lack of desire. When you are content to be the simple container of yourself, like a milk bottle set on the doorstep for the morning's delivery. When you wish you were as clear as that glass, reflecting the day back to itself. When you swoon, not into submission, but into a state of such cool transparence that you are open to anything.

The Franklin Avenue Bridge

If I walk down to the river, on a near-freezing, near-thawing January day. If I walk close to sunset, with the river white and rigid at the edges, at the center black and flowing. If I walk through the hard and the slushy stuff, sometimes gripping, sometimes sliding. If I see three small boys coming home from school, their coats flapping open. If I nearly crash into one careening down a homemade toboggan run on his front lawn. If I cross the Franklin Ave. bridge, with the moon at my back like a premonition, the sky before a pulsing, radiant orange. If I stop, transfixed by all that is passing, racing or glowing. How will I know (if I love the light at this moment) who holds me (as much as the darkness that is to come) in the world's open palm?

Casablanca Lily

White, white, unsunned white. A radial blaze of white. A flower is itself, of course, no comparison. But from your throat a superfluity of symbols—delicate hairs, spine-like protrusions on each translucent, flung-forward and curled-back-on-itself tongue; a corona of gold, scimitar-shaped seed carriers protruding from the cool, innermost chamber of green; a central, virginal stem, dripping a sweetish substance from its knobby tip. A favorite of the pre-Raphaelites. For your angular, long-necked, self-conscious beauty? Or for what no canvas, no words can represent—your air-drenching sexual perfume?

Pleroma

Such a gathering, such a picnic. This impromptu street celebra-
tion at the end of the world. The way a painter—someone like
Stanley Spencer—might envision it. Everyone touching, bodies
indiscriminate. How the dustman's wife has her legs thrown
around the neck of her lover, how the others—quite a crowd gaz-
ing on—hold cabbages and teapots up to her. No one is separate.
Not even a white dog sleeping on the grass, whose form extrudes
from the back of a woman in a flower-printed dress. As a child,
Spencer tells us, he looked on dustbins and rubbish heaps with
stirrings of wonder. For the way it would all be restored. Even an
empty jam tin—everything flying upward. Into a wild bloom of
disorder.

About the Author

Madelon Sprengnether holds an M.A. and a Ph.D. from Yale University. She also studied at L'Institut d'Études Françaises d'Avignon and Bryn Mawr. She has received many awards and fellowships including a McKnight Research Award, The Loft Creative Nonfiction Award, a Woodrow Wilson Fellowship, and a National Endowment for the Arts Fellowship. She is the author of a book of poems, *The Normal Heart*; a collection of personal essays, *Rivers, Stories, Houses, Dreams;* and a memoir, *Crying at the Movies.* She has co-edited several volumes, including a collection of travel writing by women, *The House on Via Gombito.* She is currently Professor of English at the University of Minnesota in Minneapolis.

The Marie Alexander Poetry Series

Series Editor: Robert Alexander

Volume 9
The Angel of Duluth
Madelon Sprengnether

Volume 8
Light From An Eclipse
Nancy Lagomarsino

Volume 7
A Handbook for Writers
Vern Rutsala

Volume 6
The Blue Dress
Alison Townsend

Volume 5
Moments Without Names:
New & Selected Prose Poems
Morton Marcus

Volume 4
Whatever Shines
Kathleen McGookey